Wedding Vow Book
Compiled By
Rev. Ken Owens

Non-Fiction / Reference / Wedding

Wedding Vow Book
Designing Your Perfect Ceremony

by Reverend Ken Owens
www.WeddingVowBook.com

© 2018
© 2004 Original eBook
Ken Owens
Las Vegas, NV USA
Email: ken@thekenowens.com
www.TheKenOwens.com

All rights reserved.

Published and Printed in the United States of America. No part of this work may be reproduced without express written permission.

Cover design by: Michael Corvin
Ken's headshot by: Chuck Rounds

Personal Dynamics Publishing
www.PersonalDynamicsPublishing.com

ISBN: 978-0-9890889-3-0

> For those who enjoy finding grammatical errors and typos, please know that I have left a few of them in here just for you!

Dedication

This book is dedicated to my parents, Bruce and Janet Owens who are always supportive. All my love! Congratulations on 60 years of marriage!

Congratulations on your upcoming ceremony,

It is with joy that I share this Wedding Manual with you. The purpose of this program is to allow **you**, the opportunity to design your perfect wedding ceremony. Trust your emotional responses - only the two of you can create a ceremony the way you want it. Pick one option from each ceremony section. Feel free to be creative remembering that this is meant to be a workbook to create your most-memorable wedding experience. Cross out words and rewrite sections to fit your thoughts and desires for your perfect ceremony. After all, it's **your** day!

Many blessings on your new or renewed life together!

~ **Rev. Ken**

PS. For **same sex** ceremonies, simply interchange your names for the Bride/Groom designations in each of the ceremony sections. Also, replace him/her in this manual with him/him or her/her. No gender biases are meant by the Bride/Groom labels throughout this book.

Table of Contents

Congratulations	7
The Art of Marriage	11
Traditions Through The Ages	13

Order of Ceremony

1. **Processional**	17
2. **Welcome**	19
3. **Prayer / Invocation ***	29
4. **Candle Lighting / Roses ***	35
5. **Readings / Poetry ***	39
6. **Vows**	55
7. **Exchange Rings**	65
8. **Unity Candle ***	71
9. **Prayer / Blessing ***	73
10. **Pronouncement of Marriage**	79
11. **Benediction**	83
12. **Presentation of Couple**	87
13. **Recessional**	89
14. **Alternative Ceremonies ***	91

* (Indicates portions that are optional in a traditional ceremony)

Musical Suggestions	103
Grace & Frankie TV Show Wedding	109
Leonard Cohen's Hallelujah	111
References	113
About Ken Owens	115
Order Form	116

The Art of Marriage

A good marriage must be created.

In marriage the little things are the big things...

It is never being too old to hold hands...

It's remembering to say "I Love You" at the end of each day...

It is never going to sleep angry.

It is speaking words of appreciation and demonstrating gratitude in thoughtful ways.

It is having the capacity to forgive and forget.

It is giving each other a safe place in which to grow.

It is not marrying the right person; it is being the right partner.

~ Wilfred A. Peterson

Wedding Traditions
Where Did They Come From?

Weddings: The practice of getting married has changed over the years from that of a business arrangement for social status to that of love. Most early weddings, especially for individuals in powerful positions, were not about finding your soul mate and living together forever in love, but rather more about politics and survival. Brides were often kidnapped from neighboring tribes or used as a tool to bring two tribes or countries together. In the case of a kidnapping, the couple would stay away for as long as possible to avoid retaliation. This time-period evolved into today's practice of the 'honeymoon'.

Early American weddings for people of wealth were more business arrangements with formal letters being exchanged between the groom's and bride's parents, listing the possessions of each and why the union would be financially and socially beneficial.

Over the last 100 years, weddings joining two people in love can take place: outdoors, in a church, at a home, in a judge's chambers, in the air, at sea, and here in Las Vegas in a commercial wedding chapel. Whether formal or simple, silly or solemn, with two guests or two thousand; weddings remain an important occasion in one's life.

Shoes, Tin Cans, and Honking Horns: In early times, a bride's father would take away his daughter's shoes and give them to her new husband as a symbol of her being faithful and not running away. Shoes were sometimes thrown at the bride and groom. Ouch!! Glad that has changed to flowers, birdseed and rice. In some cultures, after the wedding as the newlyweds departed, loud noises were made to scare away any evil spirits that may try to harm the couple. So, the practice of tying shoes and tin cans to a bumper and the honking of horns is a blend of these old-tyme customs.

Flowers: Flowers have always been an important part of a wedding ceremony…all the way back to ancient Greece. Flowers and herbs are considered a gift of nature and a symbol of fertility. Wreaths of flowers and herbs were often worn around the heads of both the bride and groom. Many cultures and traditions believed that herbs had magical powers to ward off evil spirits and bring happiness to the new couple. A 'Flower Girl' sprinkling flower petals on the bride's path down the aisle seems to have originated in traditions of early England.

Cake: During the early Roman Empire, a loaf of wheat bread was broken over the head of the bride, by the groom; and the crumbs that fell were eaten by the wedding guests for good luck. YUCK! During the Middle Ages, sweet buns were brought to the wedding and piled together to make a tall stack which the bride and groom would have to lean across and kiss. The higher the stack, the more prosperous the wedding couple would be. In the 16th century, a French baker introduced a layered cake with frosting to resemble a pile of sweet buns. The tiered wedding cake, popular in today's traditions, probably took its inspiration from the early pile of sweet buns. However today, a mischievous bride and groom will mush a piece of cake in each other's face instead to kissing across it, like ancient newlyweds did over the pile of sweet buns.

Wedding Dress: The white wedding dress only came into popularity in the late 1800's in Victorian Britain after Queen Victoria wore a white lace dress at her wedding. Blue was a more common color early on and represented femininity, purity, stability, and loyalty. In many countries, the more colorful the dress...the better! A bride's economic status determined how elaborate her dress would be. Even brides with a limited budget would try to have an elegant gown. Often, the amount of material in dress would be a reflection of the bride's social status. During the Great Depression, many women would get married in their *Sunday Best Dress*, rather than a costly formal wedding gown. Today, anything goes! However, a formal white gown representing goodness, purity (not *virginity*), and perfection is the favorite choice. So YES, anyone can wear white!

Processional

(Instrumental Musical Selections)

Typically, a couple classical music selections are followed by The Bridal Chorus. Here are a few musical suggestions:

Canon In D   Johann Pachelbel
Ave Maria   Numerous Artists
Bridal Chorus (Here Comes The Bride)
         Richard Wagner's Opera *Lohengrid*

Additional Instrumental Suggestions:

A Thousand Years	Christina Perri
Ariso	David B. Hooten
Bitter Sweet Symphony	The Verve
Con Te Partiro	Patriro
Allegro Maestoso	Handel
Dodi Li Traditional	Various
Trumpet Voluntary	Jeremiah Clarke
Adagio In G Minor	Albinoni
All You Need Is Love	Beatles
Somewhere Only We Know	Keane
Marry Me	Train
The Luckiest	Train
Here Comes The Sun	Beatles

(Other musical suggestions are found on page 103)

Welcome / Opening Statement / Address To Couple

2.1 (Read by Bride or Groom) Dear Friends and Relatives, it is with great joy that we welcome you to our wedding! We feel a miracle has happened here. Two unique people from different backgrounds and traditions grew-up, studied and worked in different parts of the country. Amazingly, their paths crossed. They noticed one another, and the seed of love was planted and grew. We are those people and we invite you to join us in thanking God for bringing us together.

2.2 Dear Friends, we are assembled here today to unite **GROOM** and **BRIDE** in marriage; a permanent relationship of one man and one woman freely and totally committed to each other as husband and wife for a lifetime. If marriage is to last for a lifetime, it must be built upon love - caring more for the welfare of the beloved than your own. **GROOM** and **BRIDE,** it is my fervent prayer that your marriage will always be blessed with an abundance of this kind of love.

2.3 We are gathered here today in the presence of God to give thanks for the gift of marriage, and to witness the joining together of **BRIDE** and **GROOM**. The uniting in marriage of two individuals from two separate families and backgrounds to establish a new family is an important and memorable event.

For us, attached as we are to **BRIDE** and to **GROOM** by special bonds of love and affection, the uniting of these two people in heart and body and mind is an occasion of great significance which we can all celebrate.

Marriage is not a casual event, nor is it simply a private affair between two individuals. Marriage is to be entered into responsibly and prayerfully. This marriage brings together this day two individuals, two families, and two communities of faith. It is, then, in the midst of a troubled and broken society, a sign of hope. It deserves and needs the support of a wider community. Today is a time for family and friends to share in their commitment to each other by offering **GROOM** and **BRIDE** our continued support, love and best wishes in their lives together.

In their love together, which they will publicly express in this ceremony, **GROOM** and **BRIDE** demonstrate not only their joy in the present but their commitment to share the future together. We share their joy and promise to do all we can to help bring to fulfillment a future of peace and justice for them and for all humanity.

2.4 On behalf of **BRIDE** and **GROOM**, I welcome you all here today. **BRIDE** and **GROOM** symbolize a lesson in love and harmony, encouraging all of us to seek a common bond. They come before us with a spirit of human unity, a respect for the tradition of marriage, a strong love for each other, family and friends, and faith.

I wish to say to the family and friends of **BRIDE** and **GROOM** that this is your service as well as theirs. The future of their lives together depends also upon you. No marriage can thrive alone. Through your thoughts, your feelings, and your acts, you can strengthen their bond. **BRIDE** and **GROOM** welcome your wisdom and strength to help their love grow, for it is through this love that they themselves have grown.

2.5 Dear friends, we are gathered here today to celebrate the drawing together of two lives. We have come so that this man, **GROOM**, and this woman, **BRIDE**, may be united in marriage. This commitment is not to be entered into lightly, but with certainty, mutual respect, with a sense of reverence and perpetuity.

GROOM and **BRIDE**, as you may know, no minister, no priest, no rabbi, no public official can marry you. Only you can marry yourselves. By mutual commitment to love each other, to work towards creating an atmosphere of caring, consideration, and respect, by a willingness to face the tensions and anxieties that underlie human life, you can make your wedded life come alive.

Your love for one another and your willingness to accept each other's strong points and weaknesses with understanding and respect will help cement the foundation for a strong and lasting marriage. Learn to respect your individual outlooks. Share your thoughts, experiences and dreams with one another. Cherish the intimacy and understanding that comes with the passage of time. As you enter this union, with your belief that marriage is a partnership between equal individuals with common goals, hopes and dreams, you will give your lives special meaning and fulfillment.

Today, there is a vast unknown future stretching out before you. That future, with its hopes and disappointments, its joys and its sorrows, is hidden from your eyes. But it is a great tribute to your faith in each other that you are willing to face these uncertainties together. May the love with which you join hearts and hands today never fail but, grow deeper and surer with every year you spend together.

2.6 On behalf of **BRIDE**, **GROOM**, and their families, we extend a warm welcome to all of you, and we are all elated that you could join us for this joyous marriage celebration.

We have come together this day to uphold you, **BRIDE (full name)**, and you, **GROOM (full name)**, as you exchange your vows of marriage. We celebrate with you the love you have discovered in each other, and we support your decision to continue your life's journey together as husband and wife.

2.7 It is one of life's richest surprises when the accidental meeting of two life paths leads them to proceed together along the common path of husband and wife. It is indeed one of life's finest experiences when a casual relationship grows into a permanent bond of love. This meeting and this growing brings us together today.

In the presence of GOD, we come to join **BRIDE** and **GROOM** in marriage. It is fitting and appropriate that you, their family and friends, witness and participate in their wedding. For the ideals, the understanding, and the mutual respect which they bring to their marriage have their roots in the love, friendship and guidance you have given them.

May theirs then always be a shared adventure, rich with moments of serenity, as well as excitement; vital with problems that test, as well as successes that lift; marked by a sense of personal freedom, as well as mutual responsibility.

2.8 Welcome. **BRIDE** and **GROOM** have designed this wedding ceremony as both a celebration of their love for each other, and as an exchange of their commitment to each other.

BRIDE and **GROOM**, you two are a good pairing. You complement each other. Your enjoyment of life together is more than it is when you are apart. With the love you have for each other, everything is possible. Both of you choose to see that this union is an enrichment to both of your lives. I pray that throughout the whole of your marriage you can multiply to all who know you, a thousand-fold, and the greatness of that gift.

You have told me that your intent is that this marriage be a lifetime arrangement. Who wouldn't want that? Yet, this is not so easy to attain these days. How is it that this marriage can last? A good deal of the answer lies in the love celebrated and the commitment shared today between you both. You see, love and commitment are a good pairing as well. They complement each other. They mean more together than they do apart. Surely, your love for each other can have endurance. The key lies in love, reinforced with commitment.

So, **BRIDE** and **GROOM** always be scheming, just like adventurous children, to continually let one another know that each of you is the most important person in one another's life, and that your partner is truly loved. May the love we celebrate, and the commitment you share, endure testing, and enrich with age. May you grow old together.

2.9 Today we are privileged to share with **GROOM** and **BRIDE** a moment of supreme joy in the new life they now begin together. It is not our hour of exultation, but theirs. Yet we speak our hopes for them. In the years ahead may their wisdom be increased, that they may always apply tenderness and strength to the trials which will surely befall them. May they never allow changing customs and fashions to dull the sense of loyal love and utter devotion now theirs. When new lives are added to the fellowship that is their home, may they give thanks for the blessing of a child, and bring it to the fullness of its promise by the same light of love which now glows in them. And may they look beyond the limits of their own existence to the larger family of the world, realizing its just claim upon them. For no marriage ought to be celebrated, nor none fulfilled, unless a portion of its end be directed toward the ennoblement of all mankind.

2.10 **GROOM** and **BRIDE** thank everyone for coming today. Your presence makes this ceremony more meaningful for them. They especially want to thank their parents - not just for being here today, but for being there for them so many times in the past. They learned how to love because they were raised in loving homes. They feel secure and confident in their love because their parents allowed them to be independent. Their parents are truly - the wind beneath their wings. They have shown by example, what a happy marriage can be. Although **GROOM** and **BRIDE** are establishing a new home, the love they feel for the homes of their childhoods will continue.

2.11 **BRIDE** and **GROOM**, I don't know why marriage is called 'settling down'. I think of it as 'settling up'. A reconciliation. An ending and a beginning. The most important transition of life. A step to take with joy, because at last you have become settled with yourself. Look ahead with anticipation. Together, you will write an epic. One with many episodes, hundreds of characters, a plot with twists and turns, continuously unfolding.

How will it turn out? Knowing that would kind of spoil it. All I know is that a life well lived will test us, challenge us, and ultimately reward us. I know you have weaknesses. But you are a team. You will help each other turn weaknesses into strengths. As you look ahead and imagine the adventure to come, I know that each of you has the best possible partner in the world!

2.12 **GROOM** and **BRIDE** are delighted that you can share these happy and special moments with them as they pledge their lives to each other. They ask your support and your continuing friendship as they take this step in establishing their home together.

2.13 It is my pleasure as a minister to join with **GROOM** and **BRIDE** in welcoming you to their wedding today. Many of you have helped them and encouraged them across the years in more ways than you can imagine. You have given them the greatest gift anyone can give - yourselves. Your example of self-giving is their inspiration as **BRIDE** and **GROOM** pledge their lives to each other in marriage.

2.14 It is my pleasure to join with **GROOM** and **BRIDE** to thank you for honoring them with your presence today. Thank you for the friendship and support that you have given them in the past. Their wedding today will be a moment when all our thoughts are turned toward love and joy.

2.15 Welcome to this special moment in the lives of **GROOM** and **BRIDE**. What could be more appropriate than them saying their marriage vows here among their families and close friends, many of whom have known them since they were children. You have helped them grow and develop through all those years; we ask you to continue that support as they stand together at this important moment in their lives.

2.16 Dear friends, we are assembled here today to unite **BRIDE** and **GROOM** in marriage. A permanent relationship of one man and one woman freely and totally committed to each other as husband and wife for a lifetime. If marriage is to last for a lifetime, it must be built upon love, caring more about the welfare of the beloved than your own. **BRIDE** and **GROOM**, it is my fervent prayer that your marriage will always be blessed with an abundance of this kind of love.

2.17 We are gathered here today to celebrate the union of **GROOM** and **BRIDE** in marriage. In one sense this is a very private moment that belongs only to them. But this event is also a public service of celebration that should speak clearly to each of us. During these moments together, we invite you to renew your own marriage vows and pledge again your devotion to your family and friends.

2.18 One of the most basic of human needs is that of a deep and supportive relationship. Since the first union in the Garden of Eden, countless couples have sought love, acceptance, and companionship in the relationship of marriage. This is the deepest and most fulfilling of all human relationships - one which almost touches heaven!

2.19 Welcome family and friends. **BRIDE** and **GROOM** are happy that so many of you who mean so much to them are here to share and celebrate this, their wedding day. I welcome you and bless you with these words: Blessed be you who have come here in dedication to all that is loving and sacred. We bless you and welcome you in joy. May the Source of life sustain you. May all that is noble and true in the universe inspire your lives together and bring peace to all humankind. Blessed are you, O God, for giving life, sustaining us and bringing us to this joyous event.

Prayer / Invocation

3.1 Let us pray: O God, source of all blessing, in happiness and joy we thank You for the gift of marriage, which we celebrate today. May you give **GROOM** and **BRIDE** the ability to rejoice always in their love. May you fulfill every worthy wish of their hearts. May you open their eyes to the beauty and the mystery of the love they hold for each other. And may their life together embrace and nurture the promise of this moment, so that all who know them will call them truly blessed. Amen.

3.2 Let us pray: Heavenly Father, Who is splendor over everything, Who is blessed over everything, Who is full of this abundance, bless this groom and bride. Amen.

3.3 Let us pray: We thank You, God, for granting us life and freedom, sustaining us in health, helping us prosper, and, in love, permitting us to reach this occasion together. We thank You for all blessings this day, and most especially, we thank You for the blessings of parenthood and children, for these are the blessings that allow us to be part of the great miracle of creation. Eternal God, we ask Your continued blessing. Grant these, Your children, **BRIDE** and **GROOM**, many days of health and happiness together. Endow them, we pray, with qualities of patience, understanding, and abundant love. Amen.

3.4 Let us pray: In this sacred hour, and at this special moment in time, we open our hearts in prayer on behalf of **BRIDE** and **GROOM**. Gracious God, You have made the bond of marriage a holy mystery. With faith in You and in each other, **GROOM** and **BRIDE** pledge their love today. May their lives always bear witness to the reality of that love. Amen.

3.5 **BRIDE** and **GROOM**, may you share your experiences and your feelings with one another and thereby find life's deepest meaning and richest happiness. May the covenant which you now seal always be blessed with truth and devotion. And may your lives be bound together in understanding and with intimacy so to treasure all of life's experiences by sharing them always in love.

3.6 Let us pray: Father/Mother/God, thank You for the greatest gift in the world. The gift of love. Thank You for this occasion that reminds us once again, of what a precious thing love is. Thank You for the love that **GROOM** and **BRIDE** pledge to each other today as they begin the thrilling adventure of building a life together. We thank You for the privilege of being here today and participating in this beautiful ceremony. Let it serve as a reminder to us of the deep meaning of marriage; that two people can become more than they are individually because of their relationship. Help **GROOM** and **BRIDE** to capitalize on the strength of their relationship, to lean on each other, and to build up one another during all their future days together. Grant that their love, as beautiful as it is in this hour, will grow even deeper and stronger in the years ahead. Amen.

3.7 All of us who have come here today to celebrate with **BRIDE** and **GROOM** comprise this couple's community. I invite each of you to offer your prayers silently as witness to your commitment to participate with joy in their life together. Promise your positive involvement and support of **GROOM** and **BRIDE** to encourage the fulfillment of their dreams and to support their growth together; to uphold them and their family in their marriage; to support them in times of triumph and in times of strife; and to strive, each in your own way, to help them achieve a lifetime of happiness and fulfillment together. I ask your affirmation of all these for **GROOM** and **BRIDE** by saying with me, Amen.

3.8 Father/Mother God, thank you for the love of devoted fathers and mothers, so strong and secure that it releases the center of their affections, even their own children, that they might take this important step in marriage. Grant such unselfish love to this couple who stand before you now in this act of commitment to each other as husband and wife. May their love for each other grow stronger with the passing years. Give them love and grace enough to forgive each other during those turbulent times in their relationship. Grant them also the gift of celebration so they can enjoy the many happy times they will share together as husband and wife.

3.9 Let us pray: Father/Mother God, thank You for this present moment of joy when Your grace is revealed in a special way. Thank You for this couple, **GROOM** and **BRIDE** who are pledging their devotion to each other through this marriage ceremony. Thank You for the combination of circumstances and events which brought them together and nurtured their love for each other. Thank You for the support and encouragement of their families and friends who share in their happiness during this memorable moment in their lives. Most of all, thank You for Your affirmation and blessing of marriage as life's most sacred human relationship. Grant that **GROOM** and **BRIDE** in their life together will find supreme happiness and joy. Amen.

3.10 Father/Mother God, our hearts are overflowing with happiness on this special day, **GROOM** and **BRIDE'**s wedding day. Thank You for bringing them together and for directing them every step of the way as they made their marriage plans. Thank You also for these, their friends who have come to celebrate these moments with them. Bless their marriage and the home that they are establishing together. Help them to continue to grow in their love for each other. Make them thoughtful and understanding helpmates and companions. Guide them and walk beside them during all their days together as husband and wife.

Roses / Candle Lighting

4.1 A marriage brings together two individuals, with separate lives, to perform the lifelong pledge of uniting as one. These candles before us symbolize the union of your marriage. The two outer candles represent the two of you, **GROOM** and **BRIDE**, as individuals. The center candle, which you will kindle together, represents the unity which will continue to develop as you are married. The external candles will remain lit, to show that, even in your unity, you may also remain as individuals. **(B & G light candle)**

4.2 Will all of you please spend a few moments in silent prayer, to appreciate your own blessings of love and family, while **BRIDE** and **GROOM** honor their own families. **(B & G give roses to each other's family)**

4.3 The light of these candles represents the warmth and fragility of love. As you light this single candle from your separate candles, let us reflect on the significance of today. Prior to this moment, you each walked a separate path. Now, as you light this candle, you embark together on a shared path.

4.4 With flames taken from the candles their parents lit, **BRIDE** and **GROOM** light one candle together. Their candle is one unit with two wicks, symbolizing that even in unity they can remain individuals. They will become one family, but each brings uniqueness to their union.

4.5 As they come before us to be married, **GROOM** and **BRIDE** wish to acknowledge and thank **BRIDE'S PARENTS' NAMES** and **GROOM'S PARENTS' NAMES** for the love and support they have given them. The flowers they give to their parents represent feelings of gratitude in the hearts of **BRIDE** and **GROOM**. This moment marks a major change in their lives, but the ties of love and friendship with their parents will continue. **(B & G walk to parents, who rise, give hugs, and give roses)**

GROOM and **BRIDE**, as you share a rose with your parents; let this be a symbol of your love for each other's relatives. Marriage is more than simply the joining of two lives. It is the marriage of two families. May your love for them, as well as their love for you, live on, by God's grace.

Will the parents of **BRIDE** and **GROOM** please affirm your blessings, support and encouragement. I remind you that, although each of them will remain a part of your separate heritage, they are no longer your separate children. **BRIDE** and **GROOM** are here, before Almighty God, to become one. Therefore, I now ask you, "do you offer your blessings and loving support of this marriage?"

4.6 **GROOM** and **BRIDE**, will each of you now take a candle to symbolize your individual lives. Now use these candles to light the central candle as a symbol of the new relationship you are beginning today. Let me remind you that marriage doesn't wipe out our separate identity as individuals. But it does enrich all our natural skills and abilities by helping us to grow and develop. Each of you will contribute your very best to your marriage, you will become as one in life's most intimate and fulfilling relationship. This is my prayer for both of you as you begin this exciting journey together.

4.7 Marriage brings two people into a unique relationship. In their union they share many experiences as if they were one person. But, each member of this relationship also retains their own identity. Genuine love allows us to overcome our sense of loneliness and isolation yet promises us our uniqueness as individuals. The beautiful paradox of marriage is that two people become as one. ***(Bride and Groom light the Unity Candle(s)* and yet they remain as two individuals.** *Bride and Groom place their individual candle, still burning back down)*

4.8 **BRIDE**, Each candle before us represents the eternal flame of life. Today we pray that God will forever keep our flame of love alive, and warm our souls with peace and unity. **GROOM**, We pray for hearts continually aglow with love, hopes constantly alive and free. May we always be responsive to the wishes of God, living each day in His sight and under His hand.

As I light this candle, I **GROOM**, promise you, **BRIDE** that my love will live for you as long as the eternal flame of God warms the souls of his people on earth. From this moment on, I will stand, walk and live by your side and in the light of the Lord. ***[Repeat this section twice switching names so each says to one another]***

4.9 This occasion is a special kind of celebration for the parents who raised **GROOM** and **BRIDE**. Today you are witnessing another stage in the lives of your son and daughter. Your continuing support and encouragement as parents will be needed as GROOM and BRIDE unite in marriage and set about the task of building a home of their own.

GROOM's PARENTS and **BRIDE's PARENTS**, are you willing to bless and support this marriage with your love and concern?

(Response) "WE ARE."

Scripture Readings / Poetry
(Selected by Minister and/or couple)

5.1 I may be able to speak the languages of men and even of angels, but if I have no love, my speech is no more than a noisy gong or a clanging bell. I may have the gift of inspired preaching; I may have all knowledge and understand all secrets; I may have all the faith needed to move mountains, but if I have no love, I am nothing. I may give away everything I have, and even give up my body to be burned, but if I have no love, this does no good.

"Love is patient and kind, it is not jealous or conceited or proud; love is not ill-mannered or selfish or irritable; love does not keep a record of wrongs; love is not happy with evil but is happy with the truth. Love never gives up, and its faith, hope, and patience never fail." (I Cor 13:1–7)

5.2 Eternal God, creator and preserver of all life, author of salvation, and giver of all grace: Look with favor upon the world you have made, and for which your Son gave his life, and especially upon this man and this woman whom you make one flesh in Holy Matrimony.

Give them wisdom and devotion in the ordering of their common life, that each may be to the other a strength in need, a counselor in perplexity, a comfort in sorrow, and a companion in joy.

Grant that their will may be so knit together in Your will, and their spirits in Your Spirit, that they may grow in love and peace with You and one another all the days of their life.

Give them grace when they hurt each other, to recognize and acknowledge their fault, and to seek each other's forgiveness and yours.

Make their life together a sign of Christ's love to this world, that unity may overcome estrangements, forgiveness heal guilt, and joy conquer despair.

Bestow upon them the gift and heritage of children, and the grace to bring them up. Give them such fulfillment of their mutual affection that they may reach out in love and concern for others.

Grant that all married persons who have witnessed these vows may find their lives strengthened and their loyalties confirmed. (from *The Book of Common Prayer*)

5.3 You have become mine forever. Yes, we have become partners. I have become yours. Hereafter, I cannot live without you. Do not live without me. Let us share the joys. We are word and meaning, united. You are thought, and I am sound.

May the nights be honey-sweet for us; may the mornings be honey-sweet for us; may the earth be honey-sweet for us; may the heavens be honey-sweet for us.

May the plants be honey-sweet for us; may the sun be all honey for us; may the cows yield us honey-sweet milk!

As the heavens are stable, as the earth is stable, as the mountains are stable, as the whole universe is stable, so may our union be permanently settled. (from the Hindu Marriage Ritual of *Seven Steps*)

5.4 Nothing happens without a cause. The union of this man and woman has not come about accidentally but is the foreordained result of many past lives. This tie can therefore not be broken or dissolved.

In the future, happy occasions will come as surely as the morning. Difficult times will come as surely as night. When things go joyously, meditate according to the Buddhist tradition. When things go badly, meditate. Meditation in the manner of the Compassionate Buddha will guide your life.

To say the words "love and compassion" is easy. But to accept that love and compassion are built upon patience and perseverance is not easy. Your marriage will be firm and lasting if you remember this. (Buddhist Marriage Homily)

5.5 The Old Song And Dance:
You, because you love me, hold
Fast to me, caress me, be

Quiet and kind, comfort me
With stillness, say nothing at all.
You, because I love you, I
Am strong for you, I uphold
You. The water is alive
Around us. Living water
Runs in the cut earth between
Us. You, my bride, your voice speaks
Over the water to me.
Your hands, your solemn arms,
Cross the water and hold me.
Your body is beautiful.
It speaks across the water.
Bride, sweeter than honey, glad
of heart, or hearts beat across
The bridge of our arms. Our speech
Is speech of the joy in the night
Of gladness. Our words live.
Our words are children dancing
Forth from us like stars on water.
My bride, my well beloved,
Sweeter than honey, than ripe fruit,
Solemn, grave, a flying bird,
Hold me. Be quiet and kind.
I love you. Be good to me.
I am strong for you. I uphold
You. the dawn of ten thousand
Dawns is afire in the sky.
The water flows in the earth.
The children laugh in the air. (Kenneth Rexroth)

5.6 There are three signs which warm my heart and are beautiful in the eyes of the Lord and of men: concord among brothers, friendship among neighbors, and a man and wife who are inseparable. (from *The Wisdom of Ben Sira*, Ch 25, verse 1)

5.7   My true love hath my heart and I have his,
By just exchange one for another given;
I hold his dear and mine he cannot miss;
There never was a better bargain driven;
My true love hath my heart and I have his.
   My heart in me keeps him and me in one;
My heart in him his thoughts and senses guides;
He loves my heart for once it was his own;
I cherish his because in me it bides;
My true love hath my heart and I have his.
(Sir Phillip Sidney *My True Love Hath My Heart*)

5.8   Take a lump of clay, wet it, pat it, and make an image of me, and an image of you. Then smash them, crash them, and add a little water. Break them and remake them into an image of you, and an image of me. Then in my clay, there's a little of you, and in your clay, there's a little of me. And nothing ever shall us sever. Living, we'll sleep in the same quilt, and dead, we'll be buried together.
(Kuan Tao-Shen)

5.9   My love to my husband was not only a matrimonial love, as betwixt man and wife, but a natural love, as the love of brethren, parents, and children, also a sympathetical love, as the love of friends, likewise a customary love, as the love of acquaintances, a loyal love, as the love of a subject, an obedient love, as the love to virtue, an uniting love, as the love of soul and body, a pious love, as the love to heaven, all which several loves did meet and intermix, making one mass of love.
(Author Unknown)

5.10 What greater thing is there for two human souls than to feel that they are joined, to strengthen each other, to be at one with each other in silent unspeakable memories. (George Eliott)

5.11 In marriage the loving husband or wife vows fidelity first of all to the other at the same time as to his or her true self...the fidelity of the married couple is acceptance of one's fellow-creature, a willingness to take the other as he or she is in his or her intimate particularity. Let me insist that fidelity in marriage cannot be merely that negative attitude so frequently imagined; it must be active. To be content not to deceive one's wife or husband would be in indication of indigence, not one of love. Fidelity demands far more: it wants the good of the beloved, and when it acts in behalf of that good it is creating in its own presence the neighbor. And it is by this roundabout way through the other that the self rises into being a person beyond its own happiness. Thus, as persons, a married couple are mutual creations, and to become persons is the double achievement of 'active love'. What denies both the individual and his natural egoism is what constructs a person. At this point faithfulness in marriage is discovered to be the law of a new life. (Denis de Rougemony from *Love in the Western World*)

5.12 And Ruth said, Entreat me not to leave thee, or to return from following after thee; for whither thou goest, I will go; and where thou lodgest, I will lodge; they people shall be my people, and thy God my God; Where thou diest, will I die, and there will I be buried; the Lord do so to me, and more also, if ought but death part thee and me. (Ruth 1:16–17)

5.13 The essence of a good marriage is respect for each other's personality combined with that deep intimacy, physical, mental, and spiritual, which makes a serious love between man and woman the most fructifying of all human experiences. Such love, like everything that is great and precious, demands its own morality, and frequently entails a sacrifice of the less to the greater; but such sacrifice must be voluntary, for, where it is not, it will destroy the very basis of the love for the sake of which it is made. (Bertrand Russell from *Marriage and Morals*)

5.14   You are my husband/you are my wife,
My feet shall run because of you.
My feet, dance because of you.
My heart shall beat because of you.
My eyes, see because of you.
My mind, think because of you.
And I shall love because of you.
(Eskimo love song)

5.15 TO THE WEST. Over there are the mountains. May you see them as long as you live, for from them you receive sweet pine for incense.

TO THE NORTH. Strength will come from the North. May you look for many years upon the Star that never moves.

TO THE EAST. Old age will come from below, from where comes the light of the Sun.

TO THE SOUTH. May warm winds of the South bring you food.

(Blackfoot prayer to the four directions)

5.16 I want to paint men and women with that something of the eternal which the halo used to symbolize...to express the love of two lovers by a wedding of two complementary colors, their mingling and opposition, the mysterious vibration of kindred tones. to express the thought of a brow by the radiance of a light tone against a somber background. To express hope by some star, the eagerness of a soul by a sunset radiance. (Vincent Van Gogh from a letter to his brother, Theo)

5.17 May the wind be always at your back.
May the road rise up to meet you.
May the sun shine warm on your face,
The rains fall soft on your fields.
Until we meet again, may the Lord
Hold you in the hollow of his hand.
(Old Irish Blessing)

5.18 Libations! Libations!
To the protective spirits on High!
To the wandering spirits below!
To the spirits of the mountains,

To the spirits of the valleys,
To the spirits of the East,
To the spirits of the West,
To the spirits of the North,
To the spirits of the South,
To the bride and groom, together, libation!

May the spirits on high, as well as the spirits below, fill you with grace!

Divine helpers, come! Keep watch all night! Rather than see the groom so much as damage his toenail, may the good spirits go ahead of him. May the bride not so much as damage her fingernail! The good spirits will be their cushions so that not a hair of their heads shall be harmed.

And you, all you good wedding guests waiting in the shadows, come out into the light! May the light follow you!   (African wedding benediction)

5.19 Submit yourselves to one another because of your reverence for Christ. Wives, submit yourselves to your husbands as to the Lord. For a husband has authority over his wife just as Christ has authority over the Church; and Christ is himself the Savior of the Church. And so, wives must submit themselves completely to their husbands just as the Church submits itself to Christ.

Husbands, love your wives just as Christ loved the Church and gave his life for it. He did this to dedicate the Church to God by his word, after making it clean by washing it in water, in order to present the church to himself in all its beauty pure and faultless, without spot or wrinkle or any other imperfection. Men ought to love their wives just as they love their own bodies. A man who loves his wife loves himself. No one ever hates his own body. Instead, he feeds it and takes care of it, just as Christ does the church, for we are members of his body. As the scripture says, "For this reason a man will leave his father and mother and unite with his wife, and the two will become one."

There is a deep secret truth revealed in this scripture, which I understand as applying to Christ and the Church. But it also applies to you; every husband must love his wife as himself, and every wife must respect her husband. (Ephes. 5:21-23)

5.20 Original human nature was not like the present but different. The sexes were not two as they are now but originally three in number; there was man, woman and the union of the two. The man was originally the child of the sun, the woman of the earth and the man-woman of the moon, which is made up of sun and earth. Now when one of them meets his other half, the actual half of himself, the pair are lost in an amazement of love and friendship and intimacy - these are the people who pass their whole lives together. The reason is that human nature was originally one and we were a whole, and the desire and pursuit of the whole is called love. (Aristophanes, quoted in Plato, from the *Symposium* translation by Benjamin Jowen)

5.21 Give All To Love:
Give all to love;
Obey thy heart;
Friends, kindred, days,
Estate, good-fame,
Plans, credit and the Muse,
Nothing refuse.

Tis a brave master;
Let it have scope:
Follow it utterly,
Hope beyond hope:
High and more high
It dives into noon,
With wing unspend,
Untold intent;
But it is a god,
Knows its own path,
And the outlets of the sky.

It was never for the mean;
It requireth courage stout.
Souls above doubt,
Valour unbending.
It will reward,
They shall return,
More than they were,
And ever ascending. (Ralph Waldo Emerson)

5.22 Romantic love is eternally alive; as the self's most urgent quest, as grail of our hopes of happiness, as the untarnished source of the tragic, the exalted, the extreme and the beautiful in modern life. The late twentieth century is the first to open itself up to the promise of love as the focus of universal aspirations.

In the marriage ceremony, that moment when falling in love is replaced by the arduous drama of staying in love, the words "in sickness and in health, for richer, for poorer, till death do us part" set love in the temporal context in which it achieves its meaning. As time begins to elapse, one begins to love the other because they have shared the same experience. Selves may not intertwine; but lives do, and shared memory becomes as much of a bond as the bond of the flesh.

Family love is this dynastic awareness of time, this shared belonging to a chain of generations. We collaborate together to root each other in a dimension of time, longer than our own lives. (Michael Ignatieff from *Lodged in the Heart and Memory*)

5.23 In the words of Albert Einstein: Gravitation cannot be held responsible for people falling in love. How on earth can you explain in terms of chemistry and physics so important a biological phenomenon as first love? Put your hand on a stove for a minute and it seems like an hour. Sit with that special girl (guy/person) for an hour and it seems like a minute. That's relativity!

5.24 Wild Awake: People are like cities: We all have alleys and gardens and secret rooftops and places where daisies sprout between the sidewalk cracks, but most of the time all we let each other see is a postcard glimpse of a skyline or a polished square. Love lets you find those hidden places in another person, even the ones they didn't know were there, even the ones they wouldn't have thought to call beautiful themselves. (Hilary Smith)

5.25 The Beauty of Love: The question is asked, "Is there anything more beautiful in life than a young couple clasping hands and pure hearts in the path of marriage? Can there be anything more beautiful than young love?" And the answer is given, "Yes, there is a more beautiful thing. It is the spectacle of an old man and an old woman finishing their journey together on that path. Their hands are gnarled but still clasped; their faces are seamed but still radiant; their hearts are physically bowed and tired but still strong with love and devotion. Yes, there is a more beautiful thing than young love. Old love!" (Anonymous)

5.26 Us Two: So, wherever I am, there's always Pooh, There's always Pooh and Me. "What would I do?" I said to Pooh, "If it wasn't for you," and Pooh said: "True, It isn't much fun for One, but Two, Can stick together," says Pooh, says he. "That's how it is," says Pooh. (A.A. Milne from *Now We Are Six*)

5.27 It's All I Have To Bring Today:
It's all I have to bring today,
This, and my heart beside,
This, and my heart, and all the fields,

And all the meadows wide,
Be sure you count...should I forget,
Someone the sum could tell,
This, and my heart, and all the Bees,
Which in the Clover dwell. (Emily Dickinson)

5.28   Touched By An Angel:
We, unaccustomed to courage
exiles from delight
live coiled in shells of loneliness
until love leaves its high holy temple
and comes into our sight
to liberate us into life.
Love arrives
and in its train come ecstasies
old memories of pleasure
ancient histories of pain.
Yet if we are bold,
love strikes away the chains of fear
from our souls.
We are weaned from our timidity
In the flush of love's light
we dare be brave
And suddenly we see
that love costs all we are
and will ever be.
Yet it is only love
which sets us free. (Maya Angelou)

5.29   Blessed by You, Life-Spirit of the universe, Who makes a distinction between holy and not yet holy, Between light and darkness, Between committed and uncommitted, Between common goals and personal goals, Between love and aloneness. Blessed be you, Who distinguishes between what is holy, and what is not yet holy. (Hebrew blessing)

5.30 What's Mickey Without Minnie?: What's Mickey without Minnie, or Piglet without Pooh. What's Donald without Daisy? That's me without you. When Ariel Doesn't sing, and Pooh hates honey, when Tigger stops bouncing, and Goofy isn't funny. When Peter Pan can't fly, and Simba never roars, when Alice no longer fits through small doors. When Dumbo's ears are small, and happily ever after isn't true. Even then, I won't stop loving you. (Unknown)

5.31 At The Threshold of Marriage:
The Threshold of marriage at which you are standing,
With faith you make the leap,
You pray for a happy landing,
And the rewards that you will reap.
For marriage has its own rewards,
Deep love, closeness, and caring,
No more "I" it is "us" – no more "me" it is "we",
And somehow you look forward to sharing.
For marriage can be a mystery,
How it can make two into one,
How only one person can steal your heart,
And become your stars, moon and sun.
So, step over that threshold with stars in your eyes,
As you happily say, "I do",
You are truly blest to have found true love,
And may every joy in life come to you.
(Barbara Winters)

Vows

6.1 Please turn to each other, take one another's hand. **GROOM**, please repeat after me: **BRIDE**, I love you. And I look forward to being your friend and companion, your husband and lover for life. I promise to love you and respect you; to stand by you and be faithful to you; to be open and honest with you; and to always work toward our mutual growth. I promise this with the help of God, for the good times and the troubled times, till death do us part.

BRIDE, please repeat after me: **GROOM**, I love you. And I look forward to being your friend and companion, your wife and lover for life. I promise to love you and respect you; to stand by you and be faithful to you; to be open and honest with you; and to always work toward our mutual growth. I promise this with the help of God, for the good times and the troubled times, till death do us part.

6.2 Please turn to each other, take one another's hand. **BRIDE, GROOM,** please state your intent to enter into this union by expressing your vows to one another. **GROOM**, repeat after me: "I promise, **BRIDE**, before family and friends, to commit my love to you; to respect your individuality; to be with you through life's changes; and to nurture and strengthen the love between us, as long as we both shall live."

BRIDE, repeat after me: "I promise, **GROOM**, before family and friends, to commit my love to you; to respect your individuality; to be with you through life's changes; and to nurture and strengthen the love between us, as long as we both shall live."

6.3 Please turn to each other, take one another's hand. **GROOM**, please repeat after me: I, **GROOM**, choose you, **BRIDE**, to be my wife, my friend, and my lover; to love, respect, and trust you; to support you and help you grow; to share my life with you forever, as together we work to improve this world for our brothers and sisters and for our children.

BRIDE, please repeat after me: I, **BRIDE**, choose you, **GROOM**, to be my husband, my friend, and my lover; to love, respect, and trust you; to support you and help you grow; to share my life with you forever, as together we work to improve this world for our brothers and sisters and for our children.

6.4 **BRIDE** and **GROOM**, have you come here freely and without reservation to give yourselves to each other in marriage? Will you love and honor each other as man and wife for the rest of your lives? Will you accept children lovingly from God and bring them up according to His Law?

Since it is your intention to enter into the marriage, join your right hands and declare your consent before God. I, **GROOM**, take you, **BRIDE**, to be my wife. I promise to be true to you in good times and in bad, in sickness and in health. I will love you and honor you all the days of my life.

I, **BRIDE**, take you, **GROOM**, to be my husband. I promise to be true to you in good times and in bad, in sickness and in health. I will love you and honor you all the days of my life.

6.5 Please turn to each other, take one another's hand. **GROOM**, please repeat after me: **BRIDE**, let me walk beside you in the sunlight or the rain; let me share your joys and triumphs or your times of pain; let me be your lover, partner, best friend, and confidant; for you are all I'll ever need and all I'll ever want.

BRIDE, please repeat after me: **GROOM**, let me walk beside you in the sunlight or the rain; let me share your joys and triumphs or your times of pain; let me be your lover, partner, best friend, and confidant; for you are all I'll ever need and all I'll ever want.

6.6 Please turn to each other, take one another's hand. **GROOM**, please repeat after me: **BRIDE**, I take you to be my wife from this time onward, to join with you and to share all that is to come, to give and to receive, to speak and to listen, to inspire and to respond, and in all our life together to be loyal to you.

BRIDE, please repeat after me: **GROOM**, I take you to be my husband from this time onward, to join with you and to share all that is to come, to give and to receive, to speak and to listen, to inspire and to respond, and in all our life together to be loyal to you.

6.7 Please turn to each other, take one another's hand. **GROOM** please repeat after me: I pledge to you **BRIDE**, my love and whatever comforting, whatever care and aid and good company a husband can give his wife. I will live with you and honor you from this day forward. I will seek to know you well and cherish all that concerns you. I will be with you, go with you, stay with you, and I will give thanks for our love.

BRIDE please repeat after me: I pledge to you **GROOM**, my love and whatever comforting, whatever care and aid and good company a wife can give her husband. I will live with you and honor you from this day forward. I will seek to know you well and cherish all that concerns you. I will be with you, go with you, stay with you, and I will give thanks for our love.

6.8 Please turn to each other, take one another's hand. Do you, **GROOM**, take **BRIDE** to be your wife, promising to cherish and protect her, whether in good fortune or in adversity, and to seek together a life hallowed by faith of humankind?

Do you, **BRIDE**, take **GROOM** to be your

husband, promising to cherish and protect him, whether in good fortune or in adversity, and to seek together a life hallowed by faith of humankind?

6.9 Please join hands and repeat after me. I, **GROOM**, love and cherish you, **BRIDE**, for being all that you are, all that you are not, and all that you can be. Know that I am here for you, and that your pain will be mine, and your joy mine as well. All I ask is you - your love - your trust - your caring. I choose you to be my wife till death do us part.

I, **BRIDE**, love and cherish you, **GROOM**, for being all that you are, all that you are not, and all that you can be. Know that I am here for you, and that your pain will be mine, and your joy mine as well. All I ask is you - your love - your trust - your caring. I choose you to be my husband till death do us part.

6.10 Please turn to each other, take one another's hand. **BRIDE, GROOM,** do you pledge to each other to be loving friends and partners in marriage; to talk and listen, to trust and appreciate one another; to respect and cherish each other's uniqueness; and to support, comfort and strengthen each other through life's sorrows and joys? Do you further promise to share hopes, thoughts, and dreams as you build your lives together? **BRIDE** and **GROOM**, have you come before us today, freely and without reservation, to give yourselves to each other in marriage? (Both say, "We do.")

6.11 Please turn to each other, take one another's hand. **GROOM**, the woman who stands by your side is about to become your wife. She will look to you for gentleness, for support, for understanding, for encouragement, and for protection. You must never take **BRIDE** for granted but be continually sensitive to her needs. Your life and love will be **BRIDE'S** greatest source of joy.

So, I ask you, **GROOM**, will you have **BRIDE** to be your lawfully wedded wife? Will you love her, and cherish her? Will you always uphold and encourage her? Will you be loyal to her, and true? Will you honor her all her days, and be respectful of her, and will you promise to always bestow upon her your heart's deepest devotion? Will you?

BRIDE, the man who stands by your side is about to become your husband. He will look to you for gentleness, for support, for understanding, for encouragement, and for protection. You must never take **GROOM** for granted but be continually sensitive to his needs. Your life and love will be **GROOM'S** greatest source of joy.

So, I ask you, **BRIDE**, will you have **GROOM** to be your lawfully wedded husband? Will you love him, and cherish him? Will you always uphold and encourage him? Will you be loyal to him, and true? Will you honor him all his days, and be respectful of him, and will you promise to always bestow upon him your heart's deepest devotion? Will you?

6.12 Please turn to each other, take one another's hand. **GROOM**, please repeat after me: I, **GROOM**, take you, **BRIDE**, to be my wife, my friend, my love, and my lifelong companion; to share my life with yours. To build our dreams together, while allowing you to grow with your dreams; to support you through times of trouble, and rejoice with you in times of happiness; to treat you with respect, love, and loyalty through all the trials and triumphs of our lives together: and to give you, **BRIDE**, all the love I can give my whole life long. This commitment is made in love, kept in faith, lived in hope, and eternally made new.

And now, **BRIDE**, please repeat after me: I, **BRIDE**, take you, **GROOM**, to be my husband, my friend, my love, and my lifelong companion; to share my life with yours. To build our dreams together, while allowing you to grow with your dreams; to support you through times of trouble, and rejoice with you in times of happiness; to treat you with respect, love, and loyalty through all the trials and triumphs of our lives together: and to give you, **GROOM**, all the love I can give my whole life long. This commitment is made in love, kept in faith, lived in hope, and eternally made new.

6.13 Please turn to each other, take one another's hand. **GROOM**, do you take **BRIDE** to be your wife, your best friend and your love? Will you commit your life to her, embracing all the joys and sorrows, all the triumphs and hardships; and will you love, honor, and be faithful to her for the rest of your life?

BRIDE, do you take **GROOM** to be your husband, your best friend and your love? Will you commit your life to him, embracing all the joys and sorrows, all the triumphs and hardships; and will you love, honor, and be faithful to him for the rest of your life?

6.14 Will you join hands, **GROOM** and **BRIDE**, and repeat after me: **GROOM**. In the presence of God and our friends, I, **GROOM**, take thee, **BRIDE**, to be my beloved wife. Entreat me not to leave thee, or to return from following after thee. For whither thou goest I will go; and where thou lodgest, I will lodge. Thy people shall be my people, thy history, my history; and thy future, my future. In sickness and in health, in success and in failure, in joy and in sorrow, I trust you to care for our family. And I give you my faith and my love, in God's holy name.

BRIDE. In the presence of God and our friends, I, **BRIDE**, take thee, **GROOM**, to be my beloved husband. Entreat me not to leave thee, or to return from following after thee. For whither thou goest I will go; and where thou lodgest, I will lodge. Thy people shall be my people, thy history, my history; and thy future, my future. In sickness and in health, in success and in failure, in joy and in sorrow, I trust you to care for our family. And I give you my faith and my love, in God's holy name.

6.15 **BRIDE** and **GROOM**, have you come here freely and without reservations to give yourselves to each other in marriage?

Response: We have.

BRIDE and **GROOM** since it is your intention to enter into marriage, join your right hands and repeat after me. **GROOM/BRIDE**: In the name of God, I, (**BRIDE/GROOM**) take you, (**GROOM/BRIDE**) to be my wife/husband, to have and to hold from this day forward, for better for worse, for richer for poorer, in sickness and in health, to love and to cherish, until we are parted by death. This is my solemn vow.

Exchange Rings

7.1 The wedding ring is a symbol of unity, a circle unbroken, without beginning or end. And today **GROOM** and **BRIDE** give and receive these rings as demonstrations of their vows to make their life one, to work at all times to create a life that is whole and unbroken, and to love each other without end.

GROOM, take this ring and place it on **BRIDE'S** finger, and state your pledge to her, by repeating after me: "This ring I give you as a sign of our constant faith and abiding love."

BRIDE, take this ring and place it on **GROOM'S** finger, and state your pledge to him, by repeating after me: "This ring I give you as a sign of our constant faith and abiding love."

7.2 The perfect circle of a ring symbolizes eternity. Gold is the symbol of all that is holy and pure. As you give these rings to each other, our wish is that your love will be as eternal and everlasting as these precious rings. In the years to come, they will remind you of the overwhelming joy of this special occasion. May you always be as happy as you are today.

GROOM, please repeat after me: This ring symbolizes our union - for today, tomorrow, and all the years to come. You are now my life partner, my beloved, and my friend. With this ring, I thee wed.

BRIDE, please repeat after me: This ring symbolizes our union - for today, tomorrow, and all the years to come. You are now my life partner, my beloved, and my friend. With this ring, I thee wed.

7.3 These rings are in the shape of a circle, symbolizing a love never ending. These rings are also made of gold, suggesting a quality about them that is priceless. It is our hope that your love will be of such quality that it will inspire a life together without measure.

GROOM, repeat after me: This ring symbolizes the unending union of my life with yours. Your dreams are now my dreams. Your hopes are my hopes. And your love is my blessing.

BRIDE, repeat after me: This ring symbolizes the unending union of my life with yours. Your dreams are now my dreams. Your hopes are my hopes. And your love is my blessing.

May these rings which you have exchanged be a constant reminder of the blessing of friendship you have found in each other and serve to assure you that in a changing world, your love, like the circle on your fingers, is constant.

7.4 From the earliest times, the circle has been a symbol of completeness, a symbol of committed love. An unbroken and never-ending circle symbolizes a commitment of love that is also never ending. These rings represent the ties that bind you together as husband and wife. They are made of gold, a metal that does not tarnish and is enduring. As often as either of you looks at these rings, I hope that you will be reminded of the enduring commitment to love each other which you have made today. Will each of you repeat after me:

I, **GROOM**, give to you, **BRIDE**, this ring, as a symbol of my commitment to love, honor, and respect you.

I, **BRIDE**, give to you, **GROOM**, this ring, as a symbol of my commitment to love, honor, and respect you.

7.5 These rings are the symbols of the vows here to be taken, circles of wholeness, endless in form. These rings mark the beginning of a long journey together for both of you; a journey filled with wonder, surprises, laughter, tears, celebration, discovery, and joy. So, let us bless these rings with these words from Black Elk, a Sioux Indian Holy Man:

"Everything the 'power of the world' does, is done in a circle. The sky is round, and I have heard that the earth is round like a ball, and so are the stars. The wind, in its greatest power, whirls. Birds make their nests in circles. The sun comes forth and goes down again in a circle. Even the seasons form a great circle in their changing, and always comes back again to where they were. Life is a circle from childhood to childhood. So, it is in everything where power moves."

And so, **GROOM**, I will ask you now to take this ring of gold, place it on **BRIDE'S** left ring finger, and say with me this ancient marriage vow, which I will give to you word by word: By this ring, as a token and pledge of my constant love, you are consecrated to me as my wedded wife.

And **BRIDE**, will you, in turn, take this ring of gold, place it upon **GROOM'S** left ring finger and say after me: By this ring, as a token and pledge of my constant love, you are consecrated to me as my wedded husband.

And so, it is. May your rings always be the symbols of the unbroken circle of love. Love freely given has no beginning and no end. May your rings always call to mind the freedom and the power of this love.

7.6 Lord, bless and consecrate **BRIDE** and **GROOM** in their love for each other. May these rings be a symbol of true faith in each other, and always remind them of their love.

As you, **GROOM**, place this ring upon **BRIDE'S** finger, say unto her these words: With this ring, be thou consecrated unto me as my wife, in everlasting love.

And you, **BRIDE**, place this ring upon **GROOM'S** finger as a token of wedlock and say to him these words: With this ring, be thou consecrated unto me as my husband, in everlasting love.

In keeping with the declaration, you have

made, you have given and received these rings. They are a token of your union, a symbol of enduring love. May they always remind you that your lives are to be bound together by devotion and faithfulness. Blessed art Thou, O Lord our God, who sanctifies Thy people by the covenant of marriage.

7.7 The perfect circle of a ring symbolizes eternity. Gold is the symbol of all that is pure and holy. My prayer is that your love for each other will be as eternal and everlasting as these rings. In the years to come, these rings should remind you of the overwhelming joy of this special occasion when you were united in marriage.

GROOM, do you give this ring to **BRIDE** as a token of your love for her?

(Groom responds, "I do.")

(Repeat with bride for double-ring ceremony.)

Then place the ring on her finger and repeat after me: I, **GROOM/BRIDE**, take thee, **BRIDE/GROOM**, to be my wedded **wife/husband/partner**,

To have and to hold from this day forward;

For better, for worse; For richer, for poorer;

In sickness and in health; To love and to cherish until death do us part.

And with this ring I pledge thee my love. [Repeat]

7.8 I give you this ring as a lasting reminder of my vows and as a symbol of my love and commitment.

7.9 **BRIDE/GROOM**, take this ring as a sign of my love and fidelity.

7.10 This ring is a symbol of my love and faithfulness.

7.11 Take this ring and wear it as a sign of our marriage vows and of our faithful love for each other.

7.12 I offer you this ring as a symbol of my enduring love. I ask that you wear it to show others that you are touched by my love.

7.13 I give you this sign of our love; an everlasting symbol of the vows we have made to each other here today.

Unity Candle

8.1 "From every human being there rises a light that reaches straight to heaven. When two souls that are destined for each other find one another, their streams of light flow together and a single brighter light goes forth from their united being." In this spirit, **GROOM** and **BRIDE**, take your individual candles and light together a third candle which symbolizes your marital bond.

8.2 This candle, too, is a symbol of a life of sharing. As you light this taper, remember that you are still two individuals, but you now share one life. True love consists not of gazing at each other, but of gazing outward together in the same direction.

8.3 In the wedding liturgy, candlelight symbolizes the commitment of love these two people are declaring today. Before you, you see three special candles. The two smaller candles symbolize the lives of the bride and groom. Until today, both have let their light shine as individuals in their respective communities. Now they have come to publicly proclaim their love in the new union of marriage.

They do not lose their individuality. Yet, in marriage, they are united in so close a bond that they become one. Now, following the profession of their marriage vows, they will light the large center candle from the smaller candles to symbolize this new reality. In this way they are saying that henceforth their light must shine together for each other, for their families, and for the community.

From every human being there rises a light that reaches straight to heaven. And when two souls are destined to find one another, their two streams of light flow together and a single brighter light goes forth from their united being.

8.4 Additional Candle selections are found on page 35.

Prayer / Blessing

9.1 It is God who speaks: "The mountains may depart, the hills may be shaken, but my love for you will never leave you and my covenant of peace with you will never be destroyed. I know the plans I have in mind for you, plans for peace, not disaster, reserving a future full of hope for you." This is what God asks of you - only this; to act justly, to love tenderly, to walk humbly with your God. He loves you with an everlasting love. Amen

9.2 Let us pray: In this sacred hour, and at this special moment in time, we open our hearts to **BRIDE** and **GROOM**. They have come here with unique gifts; their love, hopes and dreams, and their faith in one another. May they be moved to give and share, to grow together as a couple and as individuals. May they share their experiences, their enthusiasm, and their feelings openly with one another and thereby find life's deepest meaning and richest happiness. May the covenant which **BRIDE** and **GROOM** now seal be blessed with trust and devotion. And may their lives be bound together in love and understanding. Amen.

9.3 **GROOM** and **BRIDE**, may your lives together be so happy and fulfilling that after many fruitful years, we may all meet in that heaven to which we all aspire, and you may say to me: Here is your treasure, not only untarnished, but actually glistening more brilliantly that when it was given. We have fulfilled the deep trust which you have placed in us on our wedding day. God Bless You!

9.4   **GROOM** and **BRIDE**, you shall love the Lord with all your mind, with all your strength, and with all your being. Set these words, which I command you this day, upon your heart. Teach them faithfully to your children, speak of them in your home and on your way, when you lie down and when you rise up. Bind them as a sign upon your hand; let them be a symbol before your eyes; inscribe them on the doorpost of your house, and upon you gates. And God will always bless your marriage!

9.5   Let us pray: Blessed are you who come in the spirit of love. Let us rejoice and feel the sanctity of this moment. From the very depths of our being, we pray that **BRIDE** and **GROOM** will prosper in their life together as husband and wife. Amen.

9.6   **BRIDE** and **GROOM**, now you will not know the cold, for you will be each warmth to the other. Now you will not know the dark, for you will be each light to the other. You have this day raised up a shelter against the loneliness of human existence. Though you are two bodies, there is but one life before you. May your years be good and long upon the earth and may all that is beautiful and true abide with you forever.

9.7 **BRIDE** and **GROOM**, as a collection of words, this ceremony would count for little, were if not for the love and commitment which you here pledged to one another. By virtue of being human, there is distance between you, which is both infinite and infinitesimal. Today you have joined in a covenant bridging that distance. Always remember that in reaching across any distance, you are faced with two choices; to circle the globe in one direction or to take one step in the other. May you ever seek the shorter distance, for love is as difficult - and as simple - as that.

9.8 **BRIDE** and **GROOM**, you have now affirmed before your families and friends your love and your caring for each other. You have come from different backgrounds. You have walked different paths. You are different individuals. Your love has transcended these differences. In the years before you may the richness of the traditions that have nurtured you, enhance and brighten your lives as you help to create and shape the future. May the spirit of love be always a part of your lives so that the union we here celebrate this day be worthy of continued celebration tomorrow and tomorrow and tomorrow.

9.9 May you dare to dream dreams not yet dreamt. May you find constant reward and challenge as you pursue the ongoing adventure of learning who you are and where you want to go.

May you always have a special sense of your

mission in life together, and may you never tire of the endless possibilities of exploring your shared existence. May God give you enough tension to keep you close to Him and to each other, and enough joy to make you glad you have awakened to a new day. May the winds that blow bring warmth enough to make you happy, but never enough to blow you apart; enough chill to keep you holding tightly to each other. May God give you ears to hear each other, and more importantly, to hear His voice.

May He give you eyes to see each other smile, and to see the teardrop in the corner of one another's eye before it becomes a river, and may you have a keen sense of those times when the tenseness of the other's hand will cause you to hold on tightly to one another.

9.10 Let us pray: Eternal God, without Your grace no promise is sure. Strengthen **GROOM** and **BRIDE** with patience, kindness, gentleness, and all the other gifts You so abundantly impart, that they may fulfill the vows they have made this day. Keep them faithful to each other and to You. Fill them with such love and joy that they may build a home of peace and welcome. And guide them by Your word to serve You all their days. Amen.

9.11 Our heavenly spirits - Who are splendor over everything, Who are blessed over everything, Who are full of abundance, bless this groom and bride.

9.12 It is most beautiful when two souls finally realize that marriage is the crown their love must wear, when each is ready to say to the other: "I need you. I feel my life would be incomplete without you. I know that my happiness depends on how I strive to make you happy."

9.13 Let us pray: Lord, **BRIDE** and **GROOM** stand before You today happy and hopeful, yet also somewhat scared. They believe that You brought them together and they know that You're with them now. They also know that the road ahead will have both good times and challenging times. We ask now that You bless them and be with them in the following ways:

Help them to live up to the vows that they have made to each other today. Keep their love fresh, alive, and growing. Remind them always to approach each other with gentleness and patience. Teach them how to communicate and trust more completely. Never let them take one another for granted. Guide them as they strive to hear You speak. Make them faithful to Yourself, as well as to each other. May their life together be a sign to others that people can live together in peace despite differences. Make their home a place of peace and growth where people are always welcome. Help them reach out to others to share the love and blessings they themselves have experienced. If you bless them with children, make them good and loving parents. Help them always to remember that they are, first of all, Your children. Guide them as they try to grow and to be full and complete human beings aware of Your love. And help them to step aside when it is time to let go.

Thank You for family and friends, both those present and those unable to be with us today. Their love and friendship has led **BRIDE** and **GROOM** to be what they are today. May this celebration strengthen everyone's awareness of Your love and strengthen everyone's commitment to love others. And, finally, guide those present home safely at day's end. Amen.

Pronouncement of Marriage / Kiss

10.1 **GROOM** and **BRIDE**, having witnessed your vows of love and faith to each other, by the power vested in me, it is my joy and personal privilege to pronounce you husband and wife. You may kiss.

10.2 Since both of you have joined voluntarily in this ceremony which binds you together in marriage, abiding by the laws of the State of ____ and acting in accordance with the love of God, you, **GROOM (full name)**, and you, **BRIDE (full name)**, are now husband and wife, man and woman united in marriage. You may kiss.

10.3 **BRIDE** and **GROOM**, you both have joined voluntarily in this ceremony of marriage and have been formally united as husband and wife in the presence of your family and community. And as you have declared openly; your clear intention to be considered before all the world as a married couple, and have exchanged rings and vows attesting thereto, it is my distinct pleasure to declare you now, and before God and these witnesses, to be husband and wife. You may kiss.

10.4 Before God and in your presence as witnesses, **GROOM** and **BRIDE** have made their solemn vows to each other. They have confirmed their promises by joining of hands and the giving and receiving of rings. Therefore, I proclaim that **GROOM** and **BRIDE** are now husband and wife. You may kiss.

10.5 **GROOM** and **BRIDE**, it is now my joy to declare you husband and wife, since you have willingly committed yourselves to each other for the rest of your lives. I charge you to become as one in your relationship in the days ahead. Fulfill your promises to each other. Let nothing separate you from each other.

10.6 Now, by the authority of the _____ Church and in accordance with the laws of the great State of _____, it is my immense joy to pronounce you husband and wife.

10.7 **GROOM** and **BRIDE**. We have listened today to your mutual pledges of love and devotion. Neither you nor your family and friends will ever forget this day and the happiness which it brought to your lives. Learning to live together happily is a lifetime task and we promise that we will continue to love and support you as you build a life together in this great adventure of marriage.

10.8 **GROOM** and **BRIDE**, in these moments I have heard you pledge your love and faith to each other. Your friends and family members assembled here have heard you seal your solemn vows of marriage by giving and receiving the rings.

It is now my boundless joy and personal privilege, in accordance with the laws of the great State of _____, to pronounce you husband and wife.

10.9 Your friends and family, all of us here, rejoice in your happiness and we pray that this day marks only one of many more blessings you will share in the days and years ahead. And now that you have spoken the words and performed the rites that unite your lives, we now, by the power of your love and the commitment you have made, declare your marriage to be valid and binding, and declare you, **GROOM** and **BRIDE**, husband and wife.

Benediction

11.1 May you share your experiences and your feelings with one another and thereby find life's deepest meaning and richest happiness.

11.2 May God be with you and help you grow together. May you enjoy the peace of home, of mind and of heart together. May the Lord bless and keep you. May the Lord cause His face to shine upon you and be gracious unto you. May the Lord lift His countenance upon you and give you peace.

11.3 May you be blessed with joy and gladness, vigor of body and spirit, love and harmony, companionship and love. May God bless you and guard you. May God show you favor and be gracious to you. May God show you kindness and grant you peace.

11.4 May the road rise to meet you. May the wind be ever at your back. May the good Lord ever keep you in the hollow of His hand. May your hearts be as warm as your hearthstone. And, may God bless you always.

11.5 May the long-time sun shine upon you and the pure light of love guide you on your way and may the peace of the Lord be with you always.

11.6 May the Lord bless you and keep you. May the Lord's face shine on you and be gracious to you. May the Lord look upon you with favor and give you peace.

11.7 May the God you worship be a blessing and a support to your lives. May the God you honor help make your lives gracious and good. May the God you serve be a light in your lives and bring you peace.

11.8 "May you always do for others and let others do for you...know the truth and see the light surrounding you...have a sturdy foundation when the winds of change shift...stay forever young." These and many more wishes are my prayer, not only for you, but for your family and friends as well.

11.9 And now may the Lord bless you and keep you. May the Lord make His face to shine upon you and be gracious unto you. May the Lord lift up His countenance upon you and give you peace this day and all your days.

11.10 May your love grow your lives ever intertwined. May you endeavor to establish a home that is compassionate to all throughout the seasons and the passages of life. May your home be forever filled with peace, happiness and love.

11.11 May God bless you and keep you. May God's countenance shine upon you and be gracious to you. May God look upon you with favor and grant you peace.

11.12 You are now wed. May you always remain sweethearts, helpmates, and friends. May your life together be full of kindness and understanding, thoughtfulness and rejoicing. May the years bring you happiness and contentment. May you enter into each other's sorrow by sympathy, into each other's joy with gladness, Into each other's hope with faith and trust, and Into each other's lives with enthusiasm and embracing.

PRESENTATION OF COUPLE

12.1 Will everyone please stand? Good family and friends, it is my honor to present to you, for the first time, **GROOM (full name)** and **BRIDE (full name)**, a married couple.

Recessional

(Musical Selection)

The most traditional instrumental musical selection played as the couple walk up the aisle is:

A Wedding March   Felix Mendelssohn

Refer to page 17 for other instrumental music selections for a more contemporary service.

Non-Traditional Ceremony Selections

14.1 Acknowledging The Bride And Groom's Traditions. Out of two different and distinct traditions, they have come together to learn the best of what each has to offer, appreciating their differences, and confirming that being together is far better than being apart from each other. As we bless this marriage under a chuppah (wedding canopy), the Jewish symbol of the new home being consummated here, we will later light the unity candle, a Christian symbol of two people becoming one in marriage.

14.2 Blessing Over The Wine. Two thoughts are suggested by this cup of wine. The first is that wine is a symbol of the sweetness we wish for your life. There will be times when you drink from other cups, from bitter ones; but life offers opportunity to savor the sweetness. The awareness of the possibility of a life filled with true meaning is what we toast: the good that is life. The second is that wine is a symbol of sharing. You have shared many years together, and out of this time has grown the love which brought you to this day. As you continue to share in each other's life, you will, as a symbol of this enduring cooperation, share this cup of wine.

Blessed are you, O God, Creator of the fruit of the vine.

Love is always patient and kind; it is never jealous nor selfish, it does not take offense and is not resentful. Love takes not pleasure in other people's sins but delights in the truth. It is always ready to excuse, to trust, and to endure whatever comes. Love does not end. There are in the end three things that last: Faith, Hope and Love, and the greatest of these is Love.

14.3 Remembering Loved Ones Who Have Died. I would like to take this moment to mention that here are those close to **BRIDE** and **GROOM** who could not travel to be here today, but whose thoughts and blessings are with them; and there are loved ones who are no longer here in body, but who are here in spirit. Let us remember them now in a moment of silence.

14.4 For A Forest Outdoor Wedding. In the glow of the forest, in the shadows of the trees, in the fullness of nature, I offer myself to you as your (husband/wife/partner).

May we constantly change, constantly grow, constantly reinvigorate the living thing that is our love; and never cease our efforts to reach the skies.

14.5 For A Seaside Wedding. We meet by the sea, to become one by the border of this constant and unlimited force.

And as these waters, may our love be limitless, flowing and ever-changing. May our love forever redefine itself. May our love hold within it the essence of life.

In pledging our lives and love to one another for all the days that remain to us, we acknowledge the changes in our existence, and celebrate our commitment to a strong, aware, relationship. May our love touch and enrich all those with whom we come in contact, as these waters touch and nourish the many shores of the earth.

14.6 For A Valentine's Day Wedding. As lovers everywhere celebrate this most romantic of holidays, we come together to exchange vows as husband and wife. Today we open our hearts and celebrate the strength of the love that has led us to this union.

VOW: I celebrate all the lovers who have come before us, as we add our own voices to the age-old chorus of joy, enchantment, and love. On this Valentine's Day, in the name of all who have loved, I, **BRIDE**, give my heart to you, **GROOM** as my wedded partner for all eternity. [Repeat]

14.7 For A New Year's Wedding. Tonight, marks the end of the old and the beginning of the new.

It is fitting that we meet at this point,

acknowledging the end of our time as separate individuals, and the beginning of our lives united as one in heart, soul and mind with Jesus Christ.

I begin this new chapter in our lives, with a free heart and an open hand. All of my yesterdays have led me to today; our love will lead us into tomorrow.

14.8 For A New Year's Wedding. The New Year marks a new beginning: In that spirit, may we celebrate the dawn of this marriage with fresh hopes, deepened understanding, and a quest for discovery. May we always welcome the re-awakenings that come with love.

To every new moment of growth and learning, I pledge myself; to all the tomorrows to come, I commit myself, to you and you alone, I promise myself.

14.9 For A Christmas Wedding. As we mark the birth of Jesus Christ, we celebrate the birth of our life together as well. This day, the birthday of our Lord, is also the day we sanctify our union; it is a sacred occasion, it is the day we recognize the birth of our hopes.

On this Christmas day, in the year of ____, I, **GROOM/BRIDE**, offer the gift of my love to you, **BRIDE/GROOM**, and you alone. [Repeat]

14.10 For A Christmas Wedding. Recognizing that Christmas is a sacred occasion, I pledge to you, **BRIDE/GROOM**, my sacred love.

We choose to exchange our tokens and our vows during this festive season; in the spirit of this occasion, may our love grow and thrive, ever filled with hope, ever innocent, newborn each day and holy through the years.

I, **GROOM/BRIDE**, offer you the gift of my love now and forevermore. [Repeat all]

14.11 For A Christmas Wedding. The night is indeed silent; the night is indeed holy.

In the calm, we join together as husband and wife, having left the darkness to stand before the bright light that is the love of God. On this night of innocence and hope, I, **GROOM/BRIDE** receive you, **BRIDE/GROOM** as my (husband/wife). [Repeat]

I will stay by your side forever.

14.12 For Friends Since Childhood. You have been my yesterday, you are my today, and you will be my tomorrow.

Though it was as children that we first met, we choose today as adults to spend our lives together. May we bring to our marriage the same energy, curiosity, and inquisitiveness we knew in our youth.

As we build our lives, may we remember the best qualities of that time we passed together. Never doubting each other, never forgetting our zeal for life, and never wavering from our true selves, may we draw on our storehouse of memories for inspiration as we build on our future as husband and wife together.

Today, I **GROOM/BRIDE**, accept you, **BRIDE/GROOM**, as my friend and partner. With you, I am aware of the promise of our past, and secure in our commitment for the future. [Repeat]

14.13 Previous Partner's Divorce. I, **GROOM/BRIDE**, am proud to become your (husband/wife). Where there have been tears, I will offer you laughter; where there has been pain, I will offer you kindness and love. Where there are memories, I will open to you not only my own past, but also share freely our real treasure, the tomorrow's we have as husband and wife.

Today and always, I offer you my love. [Repeat]

14.14 Previous Partner's Divorce. This is not my first marriage; however, it is my last.

For I have met previously before family and friends to unite with another soul. From that union, beautiful children were created and for that reason the union was indeed blessed. However, life and its unforeseen obstacles caused a necessary separation, and I was alone again to face the world.

Then we met, quite by accident, and you quieted all my fears. You made me a new believer in the institution of marriage. You not only asked to live your life by my side, but you wanted my children's blessing as well. You wanted my family to become our family.

I am now at peace as I stand once again before hopeful friends and family, for you represent happiness and stability for our future. You are loving, caring and trustworthy. You are kind, gentle, and understanding. all the elements I needed to make my world whole again, I see in you. For your continued love, I offer support, understanding, the willingness to learn and grow with you. We are marrying as a family, and as a family, we will not look back, but only forward in the name of love.

14.15 Vow Renewal. GROOM: As we renew our vows, we acknowledge joyfully that this is truly a time for celebration.

BRIDE: Today we join with friends and family to reaffirm our union. We do this in grateful appreciation for what has gone before, and in loving anticipation of the years ahead.

VOW: I thank you, **BRIDE/GROOM**, for your many kindnesses and for providing a nurturing, challenging environment in which to grow. What I have promised before, I gladly promise again; to love you, honor you, and respect you above all other (men/women).

I give to you all that I have been, all I am now, all I will be. Let us celebrate our love for all the years to come. [Repeat]

14.16 Vow Renewal. I have known for _____ years, the joy of sharing my life with you. Today, I reaffirm that choice, knowing you to be strong and sure in your love, true to our mutual goals, and willing to learn with me how best to meet life's obstacles and triumphs.

Nothing worth reaffirming is still and without movement, and over the years, my love for you has matured and deepened. It is with that love that I, **GROOM/BRIDE**, stand again before you, **BRIDE/GROOM**.

With every measure of my will, I give to you all I am, and joyfully renew my vows of matrimony. [Repeat]

14.17 Vow Renewal. Our time together as man and wife has been short, but the love that underlies it is everlasting. Today, before our family and friends, we meet again to affirm our decision to marry.

You are all that I have hoped for; all that I imagined; all that I could wish for in my (husband/wife/partner), take all that is mine to offer, for the rest of my years. [Repeat]

14.18 Vow Renewal. I, **GROOM/BRIDE**, renew my vows of matrimony to **BRIDE/GROOM**, my life-partner, friend and companion. (he/she) is (mother/father) to my children, supporter of my dreams, and guardian of my heart. I will spend all of my days by (his/her) side.

Whatever I may encounter, whoever we may become, I will love (him/her). [Repeat]

14.19 Vow Renewal. BRIDE: You have filled my days with laughter and my nights with peace.

GROOM: You have brought joy to my heart and lightened my burden.

BRIDE: I looked for a way to redouble my love, but was unable; it exceeded any counting, any quantity.

GROOM: Therefore, we meet today, not to expand, but to reaffirm our love.

VOW: I, **GROOM/BRIDE**, come once again before you **BRIDE/GROOM**, to renew our vows of marriage. I promise to be strong in my love, gentle in my care, and unwavering in my trust. In the name of all we have created together, and all we are yet to become, I again offer you my hand as your partner. [Repeat]

14.20 Older Partners. BRIDE: We give thanks to God for the honor we receive today as we join in holy matrimony

GROOM: Those who have lived their lives in His service know that the Lord does not deny his children when they are in need.

BRIDE: Two of his children, young in heart if not in years, and certain in the love of the Father, meet before you today.

VOW: I celebrate this gathering, knowing that it was God's will that I meet today with you, my partner for the years ahead. Therefore, I, **GROOM/BRIDE**, take you, **BRIDE/GROOM**, as my eternal partner. Let us live together for all of our days and abide by the course the Lord has set before us. [Repeat]

14.21 Younger Partners. Your love has provided me with vision and depth beyond the reaches of my years.

Now, with you at my side, my goals are clear, my hopes are high, and my life is full of purpose. I am ready and able to offer all that I am to you from this day forward.

With aspirations tempered by realism and love limited by nothing, I, **GROOM/BRIDE**, join with you, **BRIDE/GROOM**, from this day forward as your (husband/wife/partner). [Repeat]

14.22 Younger Partners. Our dawn begins at this hour.

I, **GROOM/BRIDE**, vow to cherish, respect and honor you for all our years together. May we bring the ideals and vision of our youth, and the wisdom and maturity of the time to come, to our days of man and wife.

Today, **GROOM/BRIDE**, I, who have been your friend, confidante and companion, become your (husband/wife). Walk with me into the dawn of our life together.

14.23 Outdoor Wedding. With our only walls the horizons, our only ceiling the heavens, and our only pathway God's earth, it is fitting we meet here in the garden to affirm our love.

May we redeem the promise of innocence and openness this setting affords us. May we breathe the fresh air of hope and grow with the living things of the earth all our days together.

For all my life, I **GROOM/BRIDE**, offer myself to you, **BRIDE/GROOM**, as you (husband/wife), here before the intricate and varied handiwork of God and man. [Repeat]

Musical Suggestions

Here are numerous musical options to enhance your ceremony and reception:

I Will Always Love You	Whitney Houston
At Last	Etta James
Just The Way You Are	Billy Joel
What A Wonderful World	Louis Armstrong
Endless Love	Diana Ross & Lionel Richie
Because You Loved Me	Celine Dion
My Heart Will Go On	Celine Dion
It Had To Be You	Tony Bennett
Can't Help Falling In Love	Elvis Presley
The First Time Ever I Saw Your Face	Roberta Flack
On Bended Knee	Boyz II Men
How Deep Is Your Love	Bee Gees
Save The Best For Last	Vanessa Williams
Faithfully	Journey
Part Of Your World	Little Mermaid (Movie)
A Moment Like This	Kelly Clarkson
Glasgow Love Theme	Love Actually (Movie)
I'll Stand By You	The Pretenders
Eternal Flame	The Bangles
You're Beautiful	James Blunt
Memory	Cats (Broadway Musical)
A Time For Us	Romeo & Juliet (Movie)
When I Fall In Love	Sleepless In Seattle (Movie)
Over The Rainbow	Wizard Of Oz (Movie/Musical)
Theme From Love Story	(Movie Soundtrack)
Take My Breath Away	Top Gun (Movie)
The Wind Beneath My Wings	Beaches (Movie)
Unforgettable	Nat King Cole
Love Is A Many Splendored Thing	(Movie Soundtrack)
Somewhere In Time	(Movie Soundtrack)
Unchained Melody	Righteous Brothers
Always On Your Side	Sheryl Crow & Sting
Bless The Broken Road	Rascal Flatts

From This Moment On	Shania Twain
Can You Feel The Love Tonight	Lion King (Musical)
You're Still You	Josh Groban
Hero	Maria Carey
The Prayer	Various Artists
Valentine	Jim Brickman
Angel	Sarah McLachlan
Everything I Do, I Do It For You	Bryan Adams
Colors Of The Wind	Pocahontas (Movie)
You And Me	Life House
Kiss Me	Sixpence None The Richer
Collide	Howie Day
More Than Words	Extreme
Music Of The Night	Phantom Of The Opera (Musical)
Moonlight Sonata	Beethoven
Wonderful Night	Eric Clapton
Moon River	Breakfast At Tiffany's (Movie)
Have I Told You Lately	Rod Stewart
We've Only Just Begun	Carpenters
Tonight, I Celebrate My Love	Beauty & The Beast
Through The Eyes Of Love	Melissa Manchester
Don't Know Much	Aaron Neville
With You I'm Born Again	Billy Preston & Syreeta
Never Gonna Let You Go	Sergio Mendes or Faith Evans
Here And Now	Luther Vandross
The Rose	Bette Midler
Lady	Kenny Rogers
You Are So Beautiful	Joe Cocker
How Am I Suppose To Live Without You	Michael Bolton
You're The Inspiration	Chicago
In Your Eyes	Peter Gabriel
Always	Bon Jovi
Best Thing That Ever Happened To Me	Gladys Knight
New Day Has Come	Celine Dion
Come Away With Me	Norah Jones
I Knew I Loved You	Savage Garden
When I Say I Do	Matthew West
Spend My Life With You	Eric Benet
I'm Your Angel	R. Kelly & Celine Dion

Destiny	Jim Brickman
I Do Cherish You	98 Degrees
From This Moment	Shania Twain
Hold Me, Thrill Me, Kiss Me	Gloria Estefan
In Your Eyes	Peter Gabriel
All I Want Is You	U2
I'm Yours	Jason Mraz
I Won't Give Up	Jason Mraz
Thank You For Loving Me	Bon Jovi
Warm Love	Van Morrison
As	Stevie Wonder
Wonderwall	Oasis
The Time of My Life	Bill Medley & Jennifer Warner
My Best Friend	Tim McGraw
Wanted	Hunter Hayes
Love On Top	Beyoncé
This Year's Love	David Gray
I'll Be	Edwin McCain
Marry You	Bruno Mars
L-O-V-E	Nat King Cole
Your Song	Elton John
Just The Way You Are	Bruno Mars
Can't Take My Eyes Off You	Frankie Valli
All You Need Is Love	Beatles
Everything	Michael Buble
Treasure	Bruno Mars
Isn't She Lovely	Stevie Wonder
Crazy Little Thing Called Love	Queen
Dream A Little Dream of Me	The Mamas & The Papas
My Prayer	Platters
Only You	Platters
With This Ring	Platters
I Choose You	Sara Bareilles
The Promise	Tracy Chapman
XO	Beyoncé
That's How Strong My Love Is	Otis Redding
Perfect	Ed Sheeran
Power of Love	Luther Vandross

Always And Forever	Luther Vandross
A House Is Not A Home	Dionne Warwick
The Wedding Cake	Connie Francis
Twelfth Of Never	Johnny Mathis
Go The Distance	Hercules (Movie)
This Is The Moment	Jekyll & Hyde (Musical)
Never Gonna Be Alone	Nickelback
Fallin'	Alicia Keys
Mirror	Justin Timberlake
Come Away With Me	Nora Jones
Kiss From A Rose	Seal
When A Man Loves A Woman	Percy Sledge
Up Where We Belong	Joe Cocker & Jennifer Warnes
How Do I Live Without You	Leann Rimes
I Do (Cherish You)	98 Degrees
My Everything	98 Degrees
Love Story	Taylor Swift
This I Promise You	NSYNC
Thank God I found You	Mariah Carey
Only You Can Love Me This Way	Keith Urban
When You Look Me In The Eyes	Jonas Brothers
Little Things	One Direction
God Gave Me You	Blake Shelton
Crazier	Taylor Swift
Someone Who Believes In You	Carole King
I Believe In You	Jed Madela
You Are My Song	Martin Nievera
Promise of Love	Martin Nievera
Wedding Vows (I'll Be There)	Karon Kate Blackwell
On This Road With Me	Wes Winters

Reception Entrance for Newlyweds and Bridal Party:

Crazy In Love	Beyoncé & Jay Z
Best Day of My Life	American Authors
You Are The Best Thing	Ray LaMontagne
Signed, Sealed, Delivered	Stevie Wonder
Let It Rock	Kevin Rudolf

Beautiful Day	U2
This Will Be (An Everlasting Love)	Natalie Cole
Sugar	Maroon 5
How Sweet It Is (To Be Loved By You)	Marvin Gaye
Uptown Funk	Bruno Mars
Forever	Chris Brown
Happy	Pharrell Williams
Time of Our Lives	Pitbull & Ne-Yo
Feel So Close	Calvin Harris
Bring Em Out	TI
Get Up Off That Thing	James Brown
I Gotta Feeling	Black Eyed Peas
The Way You Make Me Feel	Michael Jackson
Celebration	Kool & The Gang
I Wanna Dance With Somebody	Whitney Houston
Save The Last Dance For Me	Michael Buble
Don't Stop Believin'	Journey
We Found Love	Rihanna & Calvin Harris
Get Lucky	Daft Punk
All of Me	John Legend
Timber	Pitbull & Ke$ha

Grace and Frankie TV Show

Same Sex Service

We are here to join **A** with **B**, because they truly and deeply love each other.

A, do you happily make the decision with an open heart to join your lives, to fulfill your dreams, to embrace adventures, and create memories together? (I do)

B, do you happily make the decision with an open heart to join your lives, to fulfill your dreams, to embrace adventures, and create memories together? (I do)

Rings (Exchange Rings)

By the power invested in me, I now pronounce you married!

(Personal Vow one partner read to the other): I love you for who you are and for who I am with you. From this day forward, I freely and joyfully join my life with yours. Wherever you go, I will go. Whatever you face, I will face. I will care for you should you become ill. I will comfort you, should you feel sad. I will bathe in your joy. I am yours completely and forever. I take you as my partner in life, for life; and I will give myself to none other.

Sung to Leonard Cohen's *Hallelujah*

Have a live vocalist (or minister) sing this, with music, as bride walks down the aisle or replace the *Welcome* section with this song:

We join together here today,
To help two people on their way,
As **BRIDE** and **GROOM** start their life together,
And now we've reached their special date,
We've come to help them celebrate,
And show them how much we all love them too-ya,
Hallelujah, Hallelujah, Hallelujah,
Hallelu......jah,
As **BRIDE** is walking up the aisle,
And **GROOM** looks up and gives a smile,
The love that flows between them fills the church-ya,
With **BRIDE'S** friends and family on her side,
She really is the blushing bride,
With love and pride they lead her Hallelujah,
Hallelujah, Hallelujah, Hallelujah,
Hallelu......jah,
With the priest and the family who lead the prayers,
We say our lines and they say theirs,
We guide them through the ceremony I do-ya,
And in this house of God above,
They join their hands to show their love,
And say those moist important words ... I do ya,
Hallelujah, Hallelujah, Hallelujah,
Hallelujah,
Hallelujah, Hallelujah, Hallelujah,
Hallelujah,
Hallelujah.

(Written and made popular by YouTube sensation, Irish Catholic Priest Father Ray Kelly)

References

Father Ray Kelly: You can have Father Kelly sing his popular rendition of *Hallelujah* by downloading his MP3 at
www.amazon.com/Hallelujah-Father-Ray-Kelly/dp/B00T7FK6GM

Wes Winters: Several amazing wedding songs on his CD *Send Down An Angel, purchase at*
www.weswinters.com/music.html

Karon Kate Blackwell: Her popular *Wedding Vows* song as a single MP3 download at
www.amazon.com/Wedding-Vows/dp/B00G5PY1CC

Martin Nievera: *Promise of Love*
www.amazon.com/Promise-of-Love/dp/B00I12J1GI
You Are My Song
www.amazon.com/You-Are-My-Song/dp/B00I1MKQZI

Jed Madela: *I Believe In You*
www.amazon.com/I-Believe-in-You/dp/B079DM63SM

Grace & Frankie: Grace and Frankie is a Netflix original comedy series, created by Marta Kauffman and Howard Morris. The vows from this same sex ceremony was in 2015 on Season 1, Episode 13.

About Ken Owens

Ken Owens is an Ordained Minister who has officiated weddings, led Sunday services, counseled many individuals, and taught spiritual workshops in several countries around the world.

He is best known as a human-potential consultant in the areas of motivation, sales and personal development. He has over 25 years of corporate, small business and non-profit management experience.

Ken blends his corporate sales and management experience with his 10 years of crisis counseling and training expertise; along with several degrees in Liberal Arts, Business Management, Counseling & Therapy, and Ministry.

Speaking programs range from 15-minute keynote address, to one-hour overviews; to half-day or full-day in-service programs and weekend workshops.

Ken is the author of the International selling book **Branding Your Character**. You have seen him on *ABC's Good Morning America*, now let him help you and your staff take the first step in a positive change toward a happier, healthier and more productive life!

For booking Ken: **www.TheKenOwens.com**

Ordering Information

For individual copies of this book:

www.Amazon.com

Case-lot orders for resale and non-profit purposes, contact below or your local book wholesaler through Ingram:

www.PersonalDynamicsPublishing.com

For information or seminars from Ken Owens:

www.TheKenOwens.com

Thank you for your purchase!

For free updates to this book, check out the website below.

Also, for ministers to purchase Microsoft Word version of this book to copy/paste and insert names to print final ceremony scripts:

www.WeddingVowBook.com

Printed in Great Britain
by Amazon